VIETNAM WAR ELEGY

G. LOWELL TOLLEFSON

Vietnam War Elegy © 1993 George Lowell Tollefson

ISBN-13:978-0692241608 (LLT Press)
ISBN-10: 0692241604

All rights reserved. No part of this book may be reproduced by any mechanical, photographic, or electronic process, or in the form of a phonographic recording; nor may it be stored in a retrieval system, transmitted or otherwise copied for public or private use (other than for "fair use" as brief quotations embodied in articles and reviews) without prior written permission.

Published by LLT Press, Eagle Nest, New Mexico
LLTPress.EagleNest@gmail.com

PREFACE

I returned from Vietnam to the United States forty-six years ago. Twenty-one years ago—twenty-five years after my return—I composed this elegy. It was composed from fragments I had written over previous years.

Given all this time, the question is: Why have I waited to publish this poem? I cannot answer this question easily because, with so many mixed emotions, it took time to sort them out. First of all, Vietnam was an unpopular subject in this country until the early nineties. Then it became in President Reagan's words, "that noble cause." I could no more assimilate the latter opinion than the former.

Men did fight and die nobly in Vietnam. Others came back wounded in body or mind. This was the case with men and women on both sides of the conflict. These actions were mostly noble, as such actions always are. The combatants are not to blame for a war. It is only their duty to fight it and bear its consequences. Sometimes cruelty intervenes. War is cruel. But this cannot tarnish the bravery, loyalty, dedication, and sacrifice of so many.

Time and the loss of this war have shown America that it was politically wrong in prosecuting it. I believe most of the country has long accepted this. But we have not learned from it. And the reason we have not learned from it is that we have not faced the full implications of this bloody episode in our past. There have been many wars, many bloody episodes in the history of every nation. What makes this one unique is that we tried to impose our will upon another people through an unprecedented use of heavy firepower.

We destroyed thousands upon thousands of innocent civilian lives: old men, women, children. I saw much of it because it was my job to do so. I was a civil affairs interpreter attached to a Marine infantry battalion. The killing I saw was not the result of individual acts of cruelty. Most combat infantrymen did their job with discipline. They sought and engaged the enemy.

But there was a general policy called H & I fire. This is harassment and interdiction fire. It was rained down by artillery and aircraft upon remote villages, all in the vain hope of striking a few enemy guerillas or soldiers who might be lurking in the vicinity. In addition to this, many people living in the middle of the battlefield were caught in crossfire. For much of the fighting was in densely populated areas. Altogether, the cost in innocent suffering was unimaginable. And we, the world's self-styled beacon of civilized peoples—we did it. The enemy did too. But we did much of it. What's more, we have never owned up to it. It's time we did. It's time we admitted we were wrong, both politically and morally.

We can do this because we are a powerful nation. A powerful nation is a strong people, and a strong people can admit its mistakes. We arrived at world power as a very young nation—in many ways a nation still in its adolescence. Let us stand up now and be a nation of grown men and women, ennobled and made more wise by experience, both good and bad. Let us admit the full measure of what we have done and learn from it.

This is the reason I have written and am now publishing this elegy.

George Lowell Tollefson, 2014

VIETNAM WAR ELEGY

G. LOWELL TOLLEFSON

1

You cannot invent for yourself
a good name. The opinions of others
turn like a wheel. Vision is a cloud,
truth an unprecedented rain. There
is nothing but earth, a compost
of days and their slow intermingling in

events: first the sun, then the moon.
Into night an interpolation of stars,
vastness of space. Below the unreachable
self, down the soul's continent
is a weightedness and center, deeper than
any gathering of waters, deeper these years.

2

Nearly a quarter century has
passed since flares filled the
night sky like ghostly swaying stars.
I am alone now in memory,
rain pouring in buckets over my
poncho and boots. The damp smell
of sandbags and the rotting wood
supports of the bunker fill me.

She was a falling star coming up
to our wire in the morning. Though
the sun had already thickened, the
night's rain fell from her with
its troubles. "My husband is wounded."
I went along the path to her
village. He had fallen
into darkness without returning.
I am out on the bunker with
flares. It has been raining
for a quarter of a century.

Walking on the hard streets of
the city, granite walled commerce
enclosing either side, I think of the
smokeless laughter, the thin-aired
grief of simple country people.

They had come in the early morning
hours. They had entered the village.
Their mortars fell in white silence,
the muzzle flashes of their rifles opened
and closed searching eyes in the dark.
We answered with a delicate effluvia
of tracers, butterflies ricocheted softly
issuing through the night. The Viet
Nam Cong Hoa slipped away like dark
water in declension. A child cried.

This people is a woman. We have
lain with her mother, churning the soft
aged belly, blind to taut revolution.

Pain is a dog barking against wet
walls of lonely thought. I have worn
the night sweating, flares on their
parachutes hunched against black sky.
Once while helping the wounded and
sick I saw a woman lift her
rough cotton blouse to feed a
nursing infant, her face expressionless,
pockmarked with shrapnel, her breast
clean and untouched. Morning is a
shadow lifted from night. Through
the clear air memory is dispersed.

3

The person of my friend was
like a city, vein after vein
busy with cargo, noise and many people.

Now electric lamps glisten along
wet streets, darkness has fallen,
trains screech on rails deep underground.

In his absence I ponder the reach
of one mind, how it filtered
into corners where emptiness had stood,

and remembering the shock of sound
on a busy street, coming upstairs
early morning from a subway,

I understand the profundity of death,
its enormous rectitude
beyond the fragmentation of living.

4

I have known winter now,
the flow of rivers till they
meet an icy edge of sea.

And I have seen silver eels,
young, moving inland, pressing cold
against a forming sky in early spring.

In myself this ebb and flow has
cycled like a turning moon.
Loss and memory together lost

are moved in darkness as though a star,
far fixed in night, had touched this earth
then sifted out beyond.

5

In a time after the rains
when the land rose up like
the breast of a young woman filled
with new green and the tiny
rice shoots, Chi Lan sat
considering. The ladders of her
heart were like the smoke
of a fire going upward. "Come,"
she said rising, "it is ready."

Such was the duty of a Viet Cong
nurse, minnows in a rice field
are scattered and small. The soldiers
came over to eat what she
had prepared. They gathered about
a large crock set over a fire.
Duc Thuy, her brother, was now
missing, like the morning light
on a river, gone at midday.
"It is good," said one soldier turning,
"that you go to the camps. There
have been rumors."

Out of a smoke of brush
jungle lifts a broad leaf
of banana. The cry of the red cock
is a silver stream on the dark floor.
Chi Lan slipped without noise
toward the clearing of a village. She
had been to three camps, their prisoners
startled with silence like charred forms
the burning napalm leaves behind.
"I am gathered out of blossom. I
am wet with the former rain."
Understanding, the villagers fed
her. They spoke in fear of passing
patrols, their chatter idle, laughter
gentle, barefoot, a burning
midday heat on calloused dusty soles.

In another village, near
the shore of the ocean, where
the white distance curves its lip
on the land like an old man (hair
tousled as spray) and his flute,
Chi Lan learned of her brother.

"Duc Thuy was many years
a good soldier. He held the rights of
his people folded within himself
as a cloud carries rain. He is buried
here in the sand, a rifle
bullet having passed through him
as sunlight travels over
morning wave crests of the ocean."

Several weeks took Chi Lan back
home through a narrow enclosure of
trails. Her thoughts were a ladder
leading upward, downward fell
the steps of shadowed voices:
"The people are simple. Their waters
are clear, churned to opaqueness when
dashed over stones. The young
shoot of the bamboo which grows
serene and quick in the forest
is sometimes broken in youth. But
the blossom that weeps in my
heart, though softer than wind,
is strong where it roots."

6

Along the copses of trees, the dense
jungle, beside the corn fields,
honeycombed like the damp-rooted rice
we set our ambushes and waited.

In the morning after the killing, we
washed the night away with sunlit
patrols. The people were smiling, over-
joyed they could see us and to know
where we were. They brought us
their broken-skulled, infected, rancid corpses.
We gave them candy, placebos, the stone
silence of force. Fractured and folded in flat

fields under bombs, this peasant nation
endured, drawn to closure in a rhythm of
wounds, shadowed in movement like a snake
                         come together,
come out of an old skin into one.

7

I have seen children, the stem
broken like a flower in wind.

The look of these people was more
distant than a flight of migrating birds.

Out of the hollow fields, broken villages
I am told is some good, a purpose

gathered in the barrel of a gun or fall
in deathly silence, soft detonation of mortars.

Years later after rain, alone on wet
pavement, I hear the keening of women.

8

In Vietnam planting season is
a time of shifting worlds when the
young rice seedlings are rerooted in
shallow water. There is a rhythmic bending
of peasant backs under conical hats in
rippling heat and a heaviness of humid air.
The sun presses itself onto the land
as though an ardent woman's belly, breasts
were to envelop a man. Into fertility
the immersion of strained minds.

I have thought of these people as enemies
in war. Defeat is an oppression of humid
weathers settled close in constraint
of my soul. Their backs now bending to
new life, women in their white
cotton blouses, black silk pants rolled
to the middle of a bronzed thigh, rock
in memory like a swaying of trees.
Oh yes, we killed a number of them, but
others erupting with young, erupting
with the intensity of an alien desire, threw
off the ardent impetuous war. Let us
forgive them their strenuous strong living.

Large gray buffalo used in tilling
red soil, with round swaying bellies
and curve of black horns, are at rest
in the village. We who have plowed
in terrible furrows with tanks, raking
the green body of a nation with bullets,
are now tethered to our doors. A
quiet hum of machinery reminds us.
They too, bending to soft mud, like a
swaying of grasses, or in a motion
of love, are rebuilding their world.